W9-AAA-666

Animal Eyes

By Mary Holland

Eyes come in lots of sizes, colors and shapes. They help us in many different ways. Eyes help us find food, make things, recognize friends, and move from one place to another.

An animal's eyes can often tell us something about the animal.

A coyote's eyes are both located in the front of its head. This is true for most predators, animals that eat other animals. Their two eyes work together to tell them how far away a mouse or rabbit is. That makes it easier for the predator to catch animals to eat (prey).

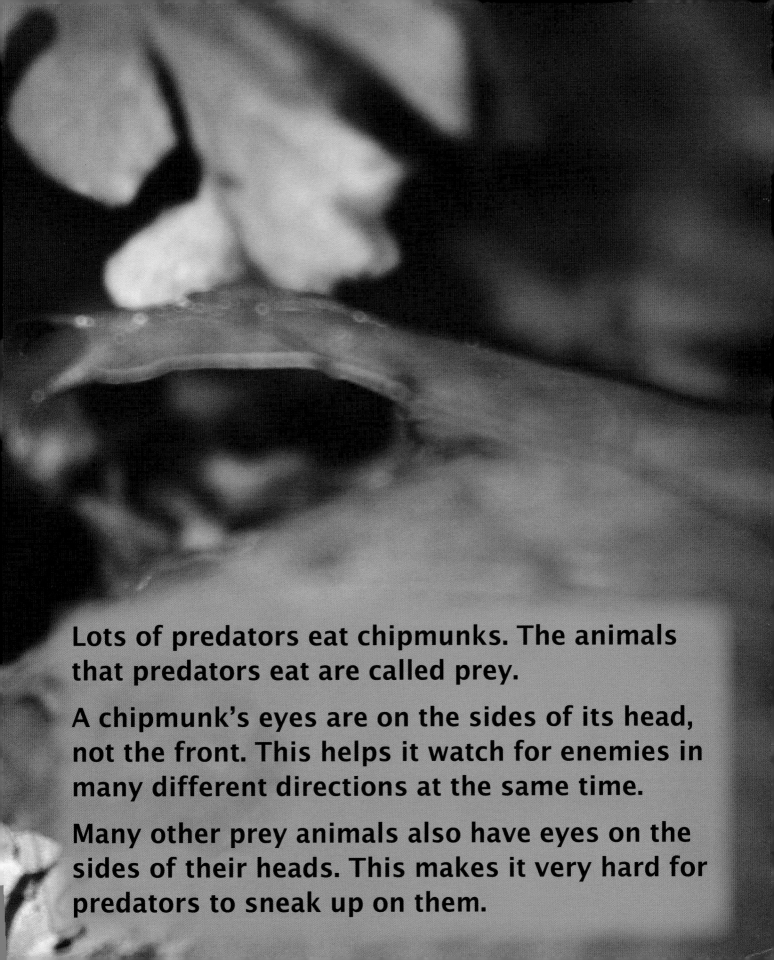

Lots of predators eat chipmunks. The animals that predators eat are called prey.

A chipmunk's eyes are on the sides of its head, not the front. This helps it watch for enemies in many different directions at the same time.

Many other prey animals also have eyes on the sides of their heads. This makes it very hard for predators to sneak up on them.

Most hawks can see even better than people. Each of a red-tailed hawk's eyes is as big as or bigger than its brain. Hawks can spot prey from very far away, even if it as small as a mouse.

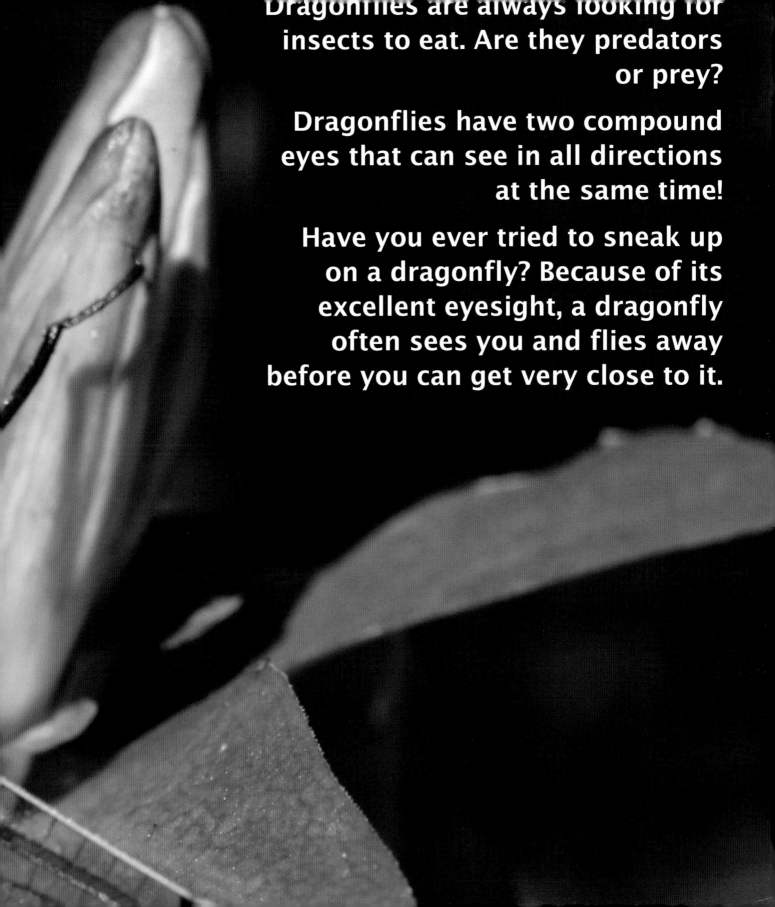

Dragonflies are always looking for insects to eat. Are they predators or prey?

Dragonflies have two compound eyes that can see in all directions at the same time!

Have you ever tried to sneak up on a dragonfly? Because of its excellent eyesight, a dragonfly often sees you and flies away before you can get very close to it.

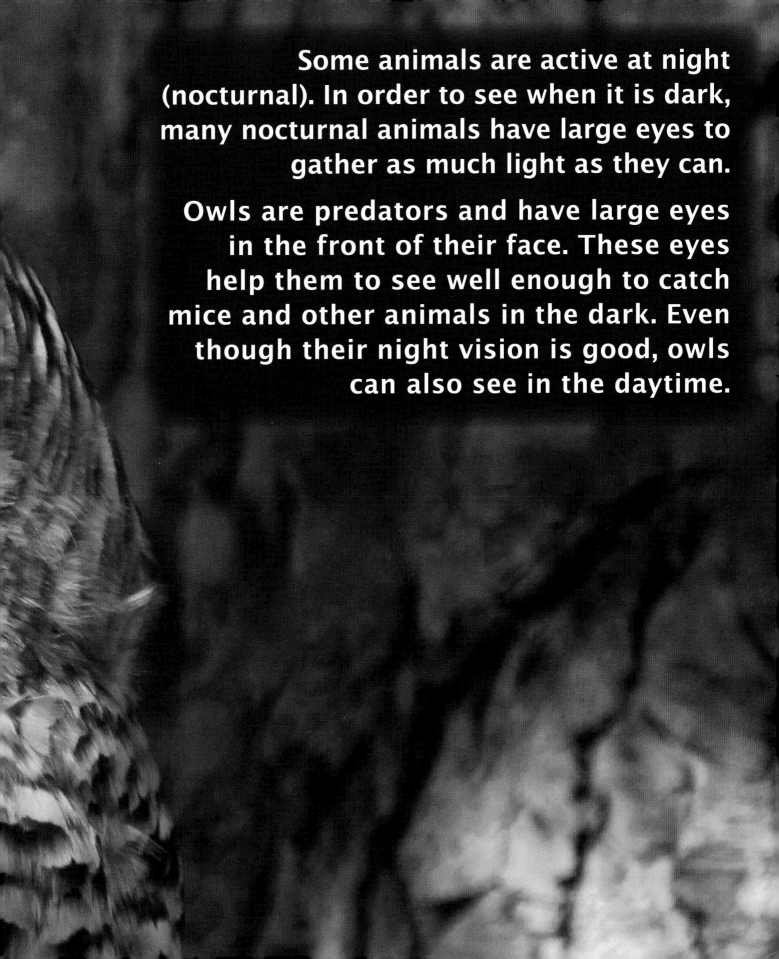

Some animals are active at night (nocturnal). In order to see when it is dark, many nocturnal animals have large eyes to gather as much light as they can.

Owls are predators and have large eyes in the front of their face. These eyes help them to see well enough to catch mice and other animals in the dark. Even though their night vision is good, owls can also see in the daytime.

Flying squirrels are also active at night, but they are prey for other animals. Predators that are awake at night like to eat them. Like the owls, flying squirrels have big eyes so that they can see well at night.

Many animals have two eyes. Snakes, turtles, frogs, salamanders, fishes, most insects, and mammals—including you and I—all have two eyes.

Most spiders have eight eyes. You would think that if you had eight eyes, you would see very well. Many of the spiders that spin webs to trap insects don't need to—their webs do the catching! Other spiders, like this jumping spider, do see well in order to hunt and catch prey.

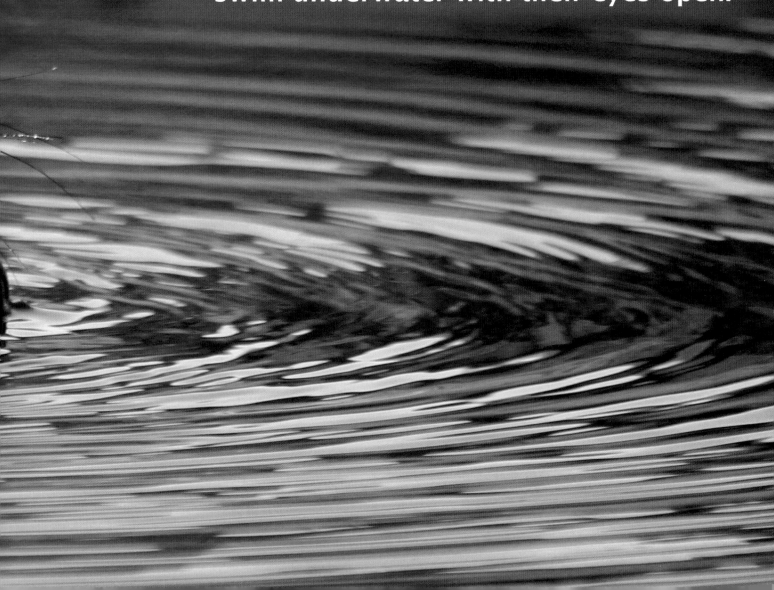

Humans have two eyelids that move up and down to protect our eyes.

Some animals have a third eyelid that protects their eyes. This third, see-through eyelid moves across each eye.

Many animals that swim, like this beaver, use these eyelids like goggles. The eyelids keep water out of their eyes and let them swim underwater with their eyes open.

Snakes have eyes, but no eyelids. Their eyes are protected with clear, see-through scales that are part of their skin!

Sometimes you can tell the age of an animal by the color of its eyes. Very young black bear cubs have blue eyes. As they get older, their eyes turn brown.

Do you think this black bear cub is very young or older?

Sometimes you can tell whether an animal is a boy or girl by looking at the color of its eyes. Girl box turtles often have brown eyes and boy box turtles usually have red eyes. Do you think that this box turtle is a boy or a girl?

Seeing is the most important sense for many animals. Being able to see helps an animal stay safe and alive.

For Creative Minds

This For Creative Minds educational section contains activities to engage children in learning while making it fun at the same time. The activities build on the underlying subjects introduced in the story. While older children may be able to do these activities on their own, we encourage adults to work with the young children in their lives. Even if the adults have long forgotten or never learned this information, they can still work through the activities and be experts in their children's eyes! Exposure to these concepts at a young age helps to build a strong foundation for easier comprehension later in life. This section may be photocopied or printed from our website by the owner of this book for educational, non-commercial uses. Cross-curricular teaching activities for use at home or in the classroom, interactive quizzes, and more are available online. Go to www.ArbordalePublishing.com and click on the book's cover to explore all the links.

Animal Vision Fun Facts

Most animals, including people, have five senses. Can you name them? Seeing is one of the most important senses for many animals.

- The largest eyeball on the planet is 11 inches wide— about the size of a dinner plate. It belongs to the giant squid.

- An owl cannot move its eyes. It must move its head to see in different directions.

- Frogs' eyes bulge so they can stay underwater and still be able to see, with their eyes poking above the surface.

- Frogs use their eyes to help them swallow food! When they pull their eyes down into the roof of their mouth, their eyes help push the food down their throats.

- The eyes of bats and moles are hard to see because they are so very tiny.

- It's almost impossible to sneeze without closing your eyes.

- Your eyes blink over 27,000 times in one day.

- Dolphins sleep with one eye open.

- Worms don't have eyes.

- Some fish that live in deep, dark waters of underground caves do not have eyes either.

Glossary

Binocular vision: The prefix "bi" means two, as in the two wheels of a bicycle. Ocular refers to eyes or vision. Binocular means two eyes that work together. These two eyes are usually located in the front of an animal's head. Binocular vision helps animals to judge distances, helping them to track prey. Most predators have binocular vision.

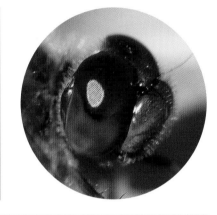

Compound eyes: Insects have eyes that "bug" out, letting them see in all directions at once. These eyes usually have between 3,000 and 9,000 optical units, called ommatidia. Because each eye is made up of many different units, they are called compound eyes. Some insects, like the dragonfly, can have as many as 25,000 units in each eye! The more units the insect has, the better the insect can see. These units are so small that we can only see them under a microscope.

Nictitating membrane: Most animals have upper and lower eyelids that move up and down. Some animals have a third, see-through eyelid to protect their eyes. This third eyelid, called a nictitating membrane, moves across each eye. Many animals that swim or fly use these eyelids to protect their eyes. This eagle has its third eyelid drawn across its eye. The small insert shows what its eye would look like if the third eyelid was curled up in the corner of its eye, not being used.

Spectacles: Snakes and some lizards don't have eyelids at all. They have see-through scales called spectacles that cover their eyes. Because the scales are part of their skin, as they shed their skin to grow (molt), the new skin has new see-through scales to protect their eyes.

Match the Eye to the Animal

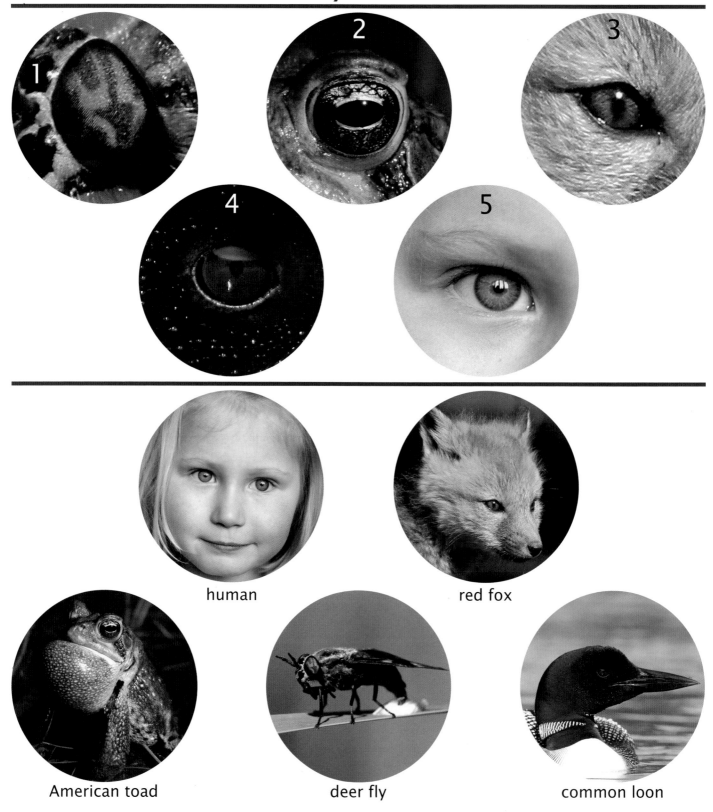

1

2

3

4

5

human

red fox

American toad

deer fly

common loon

Answers: 1-deer fly, 2-American toad, 3-red fox, 4-common loon, 5-human

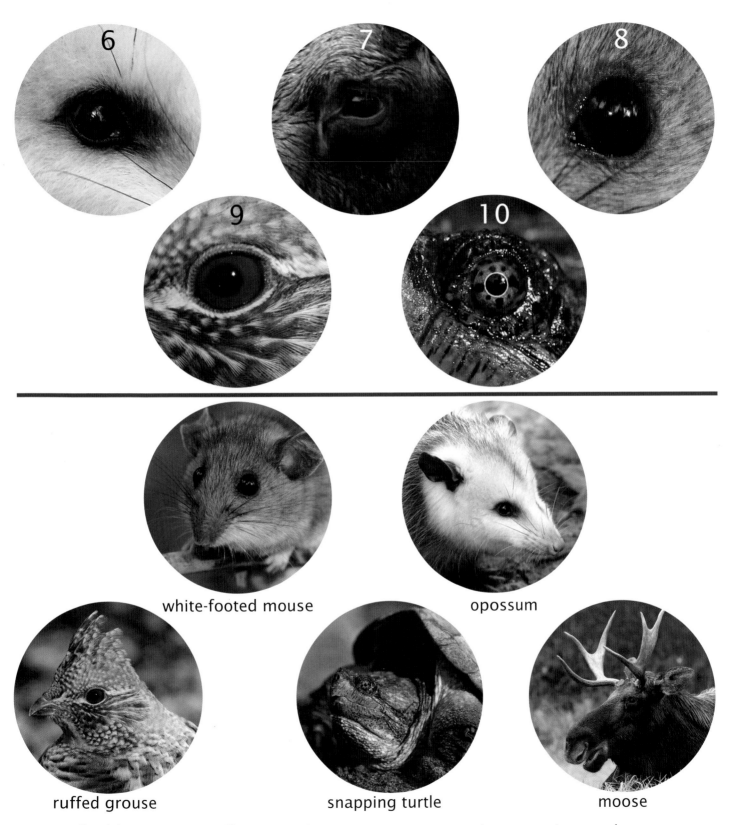

white-footed mouse

opossum

ruffed grouse

snapping turtle

moose

Answers: 6-opossum, 7-moose, 8-white-footed mouse, 9-ruffed grouse, 10-snapping turtle

The animals shown in the book (in order) are: loon (cover), slug (title page), gray treefrog, coyote, eastern chipmunk, juvenile red-tailed hawk, common green darner, barred owl, flying squirrel, jumping spider eating a fly, beaver, common garter snake, black bear cub, eastern box turtle and a human girl.

To Titus—who, in my eyes, is the dearest sister anyone could ever be lucky enough to have.—MH

Photo credit for the photograph of the little girl goes to Gigi Halloran.

Thanks to David Clipner, Chief Naturalist and Animal Curator at Leslie Science & Nature Center, for verifying the accuracy of the information in this book.

Library of Congress Cataloging-in-Publication Data

Holland, Mary, 1946- author.
 Animal eyes / by Mary Holland.
     pages cm
Audience: Ages 4-8.
 Audience: K to grade 3.
 ISBN 978-1-62855-446-5 (English hardcover) -- ISBN 978-1-62855-454-0 (English pbk.) -- ISBN 978-1-62855-470-0 (English downloadable ebook) -- ISBN (invalid) 978-1-62855-486-1 (English dual-language interactive ebook) -- ISBN (invalid) 978-1-62855-462-5 (Spanish pbk.) -- ISBN 978-1-62855-478-6 (Spanish downloadable ebook) -- ISBN 978-1-62855-494-6 (Spanish interactive dual-language ebook)

1. Eye--Mechanical properties--Juvenile literature. 2. Animal behavior--Juvenile literature. 3. Animals--Juvenile literature. 4. Adaptation (Biology)--Juvenile literature. I. Title.

QL949.H735 2014

591.4'4--dc23

2014009960

Translated into Spanish: Los ojos de los animales
Lexile® Level: 790   key phrases for educators: adaptations, senses

Bibliography:

"Beavers." *Prince William Forest, U.S. National Forest.* February 4, 2014. http://www.nps.gov/prwi/naturescience/beaver.htm.
Brookshire, Bethany. "Making a Snake Spectacle." *Science News.* October 31, 2013. https://www.sciencenews.org/blog/scicurious/making-snake-spectacle.
Choi, Charles Q. "Blind Fish Still Able to 'See'." *Live Science.* January 28, 2008. http://www.livescience.com/9555-blind-fish.html.
Eaton, Joe. "Nature's Safety Goggles." *Bay Nature.* April 1, 2009. http://baynature.org/articles/natures-safety-goggles.
"Eyes." *Horseshoe-Crab.com.* February 4, 2014. http://horseshoe-crabs.com/horseshoe-crab-anatomy/horseshoe-crab-eyes.
"Frogs and Toads" *Maryland Zoo.* February 6, 2014. http://www.marylandzoo.org/wp-content/uploads/2009/08/Frogs.pdf.
Liley, Ray. "Colossal Squid Has World's Biggest Eyes." *National Geographic News.* http://news.nationalgeographic.com/
        news/2008/04/080430-AP-new-zealand.html. October 28, 2010.
"Insect Compound Eye versus Human Eye." *Pawnation.* February 2, 2014. http://animals.pawnation.com/insect-compound-
        eye-vs-human-eye-5728.html.
Rivera, Erin. "Did You Know Animal Eye Facts." *Visian ICL.* February 4, 2014. http://visianinfo.com/did-you-know-animal-
        eye-facts.
"Worm Facts." *University of Illinois Extension.* February 6, 2014. http://urbanext.illinois.edu/worms/facts.

Manufactured in China, November 2014
This product conforms to CPSIA 2008
First Printing

Copyright 2015 © by Mary Holland

The "For Creative Minds" educational section may be copied by the owner for personal use or by educators using copies in classroom settings

Arbordale Publishing
Mt. Pleasant, SC 29464
www.ArbordalePublishing.com